Stewardship and Development

In Catholic Dioceses and Parishes

_____

Ad Hoc Committee on Stewardship
National Conference of Catholic Bishops

Resource Manual

United States Catholic Conference
Washington, D.C.

In June 1996, the Ad Hoc Committee on Stewardship of the National Conference of Catholic Bishops approved the text of *Stewardship and Development in Catholic Dioceses and Parishes: A Resource Manual*. This document was prepared as a practical companion to the pastoral letter, *Stewardship: A Disciple's Response*, approved by the membership of the NCCB in November 1992. *Stewardship and Development in Catholic Dioceses and Parishes: A Resource Manual* is authorized for publication by the undersigned.

Monsignor Dennis M. Schnurr
General Secretary
NCCB/USCC

Scripture texts used in this work are taken from the *New American Bible,* copyright © 1991, 1986, and 1970 by the Confraternity of Christian Doctrine, Washington, D.C. 20017 and are used by permission of copyright owner. All rights reserved.

ISBN 1-57455-132-9

First Printing, August 1996
Third Printing, January 1999

Contents

Foreword

In 1992, the National Conference of Catholic Bishops approved the publication of a pastoral letter entitled *Stewardship: A Disciple's Response.* This pastoral letter was the work of an Ad Hoc Committee on Stewardship that continues in existence. Since the publication of the pastoral letter, the Ad Hoc Committee has continued to meet on a regular basis to continue its commitment to stewardship education and formation.

This resource manual is the result of the Ad Hoc Committee's efforts to provide useful information and assistance to parishes and dioceses. The Ad Hoc Committee emphasizes that diocesan and parish leadership should begin any program of stewardship education and formation by a prayerful reflection and reading of the pastoral letter itself.

This manual is the result of the efforts of Mr. Daniel Conway of the Archdiocese of Indianapolis and Mr. Vito Napoletano of the Diocese of Orlando. Special thanks must be given to Bishop William McManus who worked closely with the authors in the development of the final draft. The Ad Hoc Committee is also grateful to Mr. Fred Hofheinz and Lilly Endowment, Inc., for their assistance in the development of this manual.

The Ad Hoc Committee on Stewardship would like to call attention as well to an additional resource manual from the National Catholic Stewardship Council entitled *Stewardship: Disciples Respond.* This resource manual for diocesan and pastoral leaders will complement the work of the Ad Hoc Committee on Stewardship.

Stewardship remains a challenge for people of faith today. Yet, the Ad Hoc Committee on Stewardship believes that a commitment to stewardship will enhance our lives as disciples of Jesus in today's world. May this manual be helpful to all who are looking for ways to make stewardship a reality in the life of the Church.

Most Reverend Thomas J. Murphy, Chair
NCCB Ad Hoc Committee on Stewardship
Archbishop of Seattle

I. Introduction

Who is a Christian steward?
One who receives God's gifts gratefully,
cherishes and tends them in a respon-
sible and accountable manner, shares
them in justice and love with all, and
returns them with increase to the Lord.

This comprehensive definition of Christian stewardship headlines the pastoral letter *Stewardship: A Disciple's Response*, which was approved by the National Conference of Catholic Bishops (NCCB) in November 1992.

The definition, rooted in biblical and church tradition, corresponds with Almighty God's decision to entrust to humanity the universe God had created (Gn 1:26-31) and with Jesus Christ's famous parable of the talents (Mt 25:14-36).

For disciples of Christ—everyone who responds to Jesus' invitation, "Come, follow me"—Christian stewardship is an obligation, not an option. Correctly and fully understood, Christian stewardship holds every individual accountable to God for personal care of the universe. At the time of judgment, God will have the right to ask: "What did you do with *my* world?"

Christian stewardship, therefore, applies to everything—all personal talents, abilities, and wealth; the local, national, and world-wide environment; all human and natural resources wherever they are; the economic order; governmental affairs; and even outer space. This stewardship does not tolerate indifference to anything important in God's world.

The pastoral letter describes stewardship as a way of life. It challenges Christians, inspired and guided by the Holy Spirit, to try to see the hand of God in all creation. That calls for time—quality time—and extended perseverance. Stewardship is not easy.

The NCCB stewardship pastoral, therefore, is much more than an essay; it is a workbook designed to help diocesan and parish leaders acquire a broad, in-depth comprehension of Christian stewardship. Equally as important as the text itself are copious questions challenging discussion of a total view of stewardship. Though the NCCB document is not a "how-to" manual, it has sufficient suggestions for diocesan and parish stewardship committees to develop a wide range of projects and programs worthy of being called "Christian stewardship."

For instance, the environment is critically in need of stewardship attention. Stewardship committees, after completing a full study of the pastoral letter, might consider the improvement of local environmental conditions as one of their first projects. Recycling and conservation can be excellent stewardship endeavors.

There was some disappointment, as well as sharp criticism, when the pastoral letter first appeared in print. Some thought there was a de-emphasis of stewardship as a technique to raise additional funds for financially strapped and needy church institutions. Professional and volunteer fund raisers had hoped that the letter would officially endorse donations of time, talent, and treasure to the Church and to charity as the very heart of Christian stewardship. "What we expected from the bishops," a fund raiser said, "is guidance in how to make donations to the Church a religious experience motivated by the high ideals of stewardship."

Though the pastoral letter insists that Christian stewardship should not focus exclusively on "time, talent, and treasure" for Church and charity, it did not ignore or belittle stewardship's applicability to the Church's financial needs. In fact, the letter is explicit about the relationship between practices of stewardship and the Church's finances. It says, for example, "Sound business practice is a fundamental of good stewardship, and as it relates to church finances, must include the most stringent ethical, legal, and fiscal standards."

The pastoral also says, "Parishioners must accept responsibility for their parishes and contribute generously—both money and personal service—to their programs and projects. Only by living as generous stewards of these local Christian communities, their parishes, can Catholics of the United States hope to make them the vital sources of faith-filled Christian dynamism they are meant to be."

Regarding stewardship's relevance to diocesan finances, the pastoral letter has forthright advice. "The same spirit of personal responsibility in which a Catholic approaches his or her parish should extend to the diocese and be expressed in essentially the same ways: generous material

support and self-giving. As in the case of a parish, too, lay Catholics ought to have an active role in the oversight of the stewardship of pastoral leaders and administration at the diocesan level. Indeed, the spirit and practice of stewardship should extend to other local churches and to the Universal Church—to the Christian community and to one's sisters and brothers in Christ everywhere—and be expressed in deeds and service and mutual support."

As faithful disciples of the Lord Jesus, Catholics will find the needed religious motivation for a complete commitment to stewardship. Such stewardship will help them respond to the many appeals for the donations of their time, treasure, and talent to the Church and to charity. On the other hand, involvement only in the time, talent, and treasure pattern will not necessarily lead to a full faith in all that Christian stewardship asks and expects of disciples of Jesus. A real steward is a donor to the Church and charity, but not every contributor is a steward in the full sense of the word.

The NCCB Stewardship Committee is confident that this resource manual will help dioceses and parishes conduct "time, talent, and treasure" appeals for Church and charity that reflect the ideals of stewardship set forth in the NCCB pastoral letter.

Stewardship and Development
When the NCCB approved the pastoral letter, the Ad Hoc Committee on Stewardship promised to follow the publication of *Stewardship: A Disciple's Response* with resources to help dioceses and parishes with stewardship education and formation. The Ad Hoc Committee also wanted to respond to growing financial needs in the Church. This resource manual for the implementation of stewardship and development pro-

grams has been written for diocesan bishops and their staffs, pastors and parish teams, and lay leaders. The resource manual is a companion to the pastoral letter. For this reason, the resource manual will be of no help, and might be misleading, to persons who have not first read, studied, and discussed the pastoral letter itself.

By design, the principles in this resource manual are general and flexible. They are not a detailed blueprint for stewardship education and formation, fund raising, or diocesan and parish financial management. Hopefully, individual parishes and dioceses will adapt these principles to reflect differences of size, economic circumstance, regional and cultural diversity, and local customs. However, it is important to preserve the basic principles of the pastoral letter *Stewardship: A Disciple's Response* in every local adaptation.

This resource manual offers helpful suggestions in the following areas:

1. Developing stewardship education and formation programs for adults, youth, and children

2. Planning and implementing diocesan and parish stewardship and development programs

3. Cultivating, training, and recognizing gifts of time and talent

4. Using stewardship principles to solicit gifts of treasure for annual, capital, and endowment purposes in parishes and dioceses

Stewardship as a Faith Response
With the publication of *Stewardship: A Disciple's Response,* the word *stewardship* took on a fresh meaning in the Catholic Church in America. By endorsing the concept of stewardship as a "faith response," the bishops of the United States emphasized that the publication of the pastoral letter was not simply to raise money, as important as this may be, for carrying out the mission of the Church. *Stewardship: A Disciple's Response* is an educational tool for bishops, pastors, and other church leaders who wish to invite, and challenge, all members of the Catholic community to accept their baptismal responsibility "to place their gifts, their resources, their selves at God's service in and through the Church." Thus, while emphasizing that stewardship (as a faith response) means more than raising money, the pastoral letter also enables Catholic organizations throughout the United States to develop new strategies for soliciting gifts of time, talent, and treasure that are faithful to the stewardship principles outlined in *Stewardship: A Disciple's Response.*

Using the Pastoral Letter on Stewardship
How can bishops, pastors, and other church leaders successfully use the pastoral letter on stewardship to help recruit and train volunteers and to solicit gifts for ongoing programs, capital improvements, and endowments?

First and foremost, by making stewardship a personal commitment as well as a priority for the diocese, parish, or other church-related organization.

Second, by making sure that all members of their leadership teams (staff and volunteers) understand and make a commitment to the concept of stewardship as a faith response.

Third, by evaluating current development and fund-raising practices and replacing them, as necessary, with programs and activities that incorporate stewardship principles and reflect the highest professional standards.

In the final analysis, successful stewardship and development programs in parishes, dioceses, and other church-sponsored organizations will result from the following:

1. The personal involvement of many people (bishop, pastor, staff, volunteers, and the entire Catholic community)

2. A commitment of time, effort, financial resources, and prayer to the process of stewardship education and formation

3. A willingness to trust that if stewardship is taught and accepted as a faith response, urgently needed human, physical, and financial resources will follow

II. Education and Formation for Stewardship

A Major Priority

Every diocese and parish should make education and formation for stewardship a major priority. This is vitally important today because (1) it helps individuals, families, and communities better understand what it means to follow Jesus in an affluent, consumer culture, and (2) it establishes an appropriate, scriptural basis for responding to the Church's growing need for human, physical, and financial resources.

A Lifelong Process

Stewardship involves a lifelong process of study, reflection, prayer, and action. To make stewardship a way of life for individuals, families, parishes, and dioceses requires a change of heart and a new understanding of what it means to follow Jesus without counting the cost. This conversion of mind and heart will not happen overnight, but, as always, the Holy Spirit is at work in the Church today. Those parishes and dioceses that embrace the theology and practice of stewardship are beginning to see a change of attitude on the part of clergy, religious, and lay people.

A Solid Foundation

A comprehensive approach to stewardship education and formation is essential if diocesan and parish communities truly wish to make stewardship a way of life for individuals, families, and communities. Increased offertory and fund-raising programs that bypass stewardship education and formation must be more than a "jump start" to financial giving. Such programs could separate church funding from its vital connection to Christian discipleship. As dioceses, parishes, and other church-related organizations seek to develop urgently needed human, physical, and financial resources, they need encouragement to make sure that their efforts have a solid foundation, which only fully developed stewardship programs can provide.

The Role of the Bishop or Pastor in Formation and Education for Stewardship

A bishop's or pastor's prayerful meditations on Christian stewardship should precede the start of a diocesan or parish stewardship program. Prayer becomes a potent and precious resource for the process because the primary objective in stewardship education is always a renewal of commitment to Christian discipleship. To be successful, stewardship education requires the bishop or pastor to make a complete, constant, personal, and official commitment to stewardship as a constitutive element of Christian discipleship. A bishop or pastor who does not have a solid conviction about the importance of stewardship will give only half-hearted support to the stewardship programs of his diocese or parish. The results will reflect this lack of total commitment.

The Importance of Collaborative Leadership

The bishop or pastor should convene a stewardship committee (or similar group of advisors) to join him in a serious study of the pastoral letter on stewardship. He should spend quality time with the discussion and study items for each chapter. This committee should discuss *Stewardship: A Disciple's Response* in light of diocesan and parish realities and in the context of the many economic, political, and social issues facing individuals, families, and communities today.

The bishop or pastor should personally introduce the theology of stewardship to the leadership team (staff and volunteers, clergy, religious, and lay). He should call upon them to join him in prayerful reflection, study, and discussion of the stewardship pastoral's themes and convictions.

With the assistance of his stewardship committee, the bishop or pastor should establish a series of educational initiatives at the diocesan and parish levels that would encourage all members of the Catholic community to read, study, and discuss the pastoral letter. In addition, it would be good to encourage all members of the Catholic community to meditate on stewardship themes and to pray for the grace to follow Jesus as mature Christian disciples, without counting the cost.

Model Stewardship Programs

In addition to its broader educational responsibilities, the diocesan or parish stewardship committee should have the responsibility to make sure that all leadership development and fund-raising efforts are consistent with, and reinforce, the theology and practice of stewardship as outlined in the pastoral letter

and this manual. Diocesan and parish stewardship committees should also examine and discuss various approaches to stewardship in different regions of the country. No single approach to stewardship "fits" all parishes and dioceses. In fact, as long as basic principles are honored, the more diversity, the better it may be for successful stewardship education and formation of adults, youth, and children throughout the United States.

ADULTS

Dioceses and parishes serious about making stewardship a way of life for individuals, families, and communities of faith will include stewardship themes in all adult formation and education programs. There are important scriptural and theological connections linking religious education, evangelization, and catechesis on the Church's social teaching with teaching stewardship as a disciple's response. Adult initiation processes, bible study groups, and other adult education classes should explore and discuss these connections. In addition, diocesan and parish fund-raising efforts (annual appeals, capital campaigns, and planned-giving programs) should always include educational materials designed to help adults better understand the principles and practices associated with good stewardship of time, talent, and treasure.

Leaders in the fields of religious education, evangelization, vocations, lay ministry development, and stewardship education at national, diocesan, and parish levels should develop stewardship educational resources. These resources could emphasize the integration of stewardship themes into all aspects of the education and formation of adult Christians, as well as within all levels of Catholic education.

YOUTH

Opportunities for learning about (and sharing) their gifts of time, talent, and treasure should be integrated into all educational programs and formation activities sponsored by parishes, schools, and dioceses for youth. This includes study and discussion of the pastoral letter *Stewardship: A Disciple's Response* in religion classes (both in and out of school) and the integration of stewardship themes into other subjects (e.g., environmental studies). In addition, opportunities for Christian service provided by parishes, schools, or dioceses should allow time for reflection and discussion of the stewardship implications of these activities.

CHILDREN

The lifelong process of stewardship education and formation begins at home in the domestic church and extends to parish and school religious education programs. Children should be taught the basic themes of Christian discipleship and stewardship. There should be appropriate opportunities to practice stewardship values, including generous sharing of time, talent, and treasure, as well as care for the environment and accountability for our use of all God's gifts. In recent years, a variety of resources for introducing children to the basic principles of Christian stewardship have become available. Pastoral leaders and religious educators should adapt these programs to the needs of individual parishes, schools, and families so that the theology of stewardship becomes an integral part of our children's religious education and formation.

III. Stewardship and Development

Development and fund-raising programs sponsored by dioceses, parishes, schools, and other church-related organizations should complement effective stewardship programs. No development activity should conflict with stewardship efforts in the diocese or parish. Instead, as a result of careful planning, there will be new opportunities for people to practice good stewardship by participating in the mission and ministries of their Church.

The basic elements of a parish or diocesan development program are (1) **A spiritually based plan** with a mission statement, specific goals and objectives, and priorities for funding; (2) **a communications program** that specifies how the diocese, parish, school, or agency will regularly communicate its mission, goals, and funding needs to various internal and external publics; and (3) **a fund-raising program based on stewardship and development principles** that outlines how the diocese, parish, school, or agency will identify prospective donors, build strong relationships, and solicit gifts for current programs, capital needs, and endowments. To be successful, each of these three elements must be carefully coordinated with stewardship education efforts and other fund-raising activities (e.g., annual appeals or capital campaigns) at the diocesan and parish levels.

Principles for Giving

One of the most frequently asked questions in any program of church support is "How much should I give?" The following suggestions should help dioceses, parishes, schools, and other church-related organizations encourage individuals, families, and communities to make better decisions about giving as a percent of income.

Diocesan and parish stewardship programs should help individuals, families, and communities better understand why, in the context of a total commitment to stewardship that is planned, proportionate, and sacrificial, it is important to set goals for giving. All Christian stewards must consider prayerfully the gifts they have received from God, and they should make a decision (in advance, from the "first fruits" instead of what is left over after other obligations have been met) about what will be given.

Once Christian stewards make this decision, it is suggested that one-half of an individual's or family's commitment of time, talent, and treasure be given to the parish; the other half can then be divided among other worthwhile religious, educational, and charitable organizations. The diocesan annual appeal is one of the opportunities that members of the Catholic community have for giving from the "other half" of their annual stewardship commitments, and many dioceses suggest 1 percent of a family's net income as a guideline for giving to the diocesan annual appeal.

The practice of "minimum giving" that parishes sometimes adopt as a means of ensuring that school families contribute to overall school costs is inconsistent with the principles of stewardship that encourage members of the Catholic community to embrace the spirit of "maximum giving" from substance without counting the cost. To be consistent with the principles outlined in the pastoral letter, parishes that currently have minimum giving requirements are encouraged to gradually adopt a stewardship program that avoids any suggestion of "obligation" or "guilt" and, instead, stresses the voluntary contribution of time, talent, and treasure.

Similarly, "increased offertory" and diocesan fund-raising programs whose primary objective is to increase the amount of money contributed to the parish or diocese miss the important connection between stewardship as "a way of life" and the gifts of time, talent, and treasure that individuals freely give to their Church out of gratitude to God for the many blessings received. Parish and diocesan annual giving programs should never place so much emphasis on the need for financial giving that the fuller meaning and context of stewardship would be obscured. For this reason, annual giving programs should always emphasize the ways in which stewardship influences all aspects of a Christian's daily life.

The collection during weekend liturgies can be an excellent opportunity to reinforce stewardship principles. In addition to being an instrument for making financial contributions to the parish, the weekly envelope can serve as a concrete expression of traditional giving that each baptized Christian makes during the celebration of the Eucharist.

Annual Giving

Successful stewardship and development programs frequently include procedures for encouraging annual commitments of time, talent, and treasure to the parish, diocese, school, and other church-related organizations (e.g., an annual Catholic Charities appeal).

In recent years, annual giving programs have begun to replace special events and other indirect fund-raising activities (including games of chance and social functions) as the primary means of raising money for the ongoing operations of religious and other non-profit organizations. In parishes and dioceses, this national trend toward annual giving is most often evident through annual "commitment Sundays" in parishes and through the diocesan annual appeal. In addition, a growing number of Catholic schools and other church-related agencies have started annual giving programs.

Successful annual giving programs encourage members of the Catholic community to make annual commitments of their time, talent, and treasure to support the work of the Church. Annual giving programs also promote the concept of pledging (as opposed to one-time gifts), and they encourage donors to fulfill their pledges in time frames (weekly, monthly, quarterly, etc.) that best suit their needs. Moreover, parishes should encourage individuals and families who make weekly pledges to make their pledge payments even when they are not able to attend the weekend liturgy at their parish.

A diocesan or parish annual giving program will be consistent with the principles outlined in *Stewardship: A Disciple's Response* if it is based on, and reinforces, the stewardship themes and convictions outlined in the pastoral letter. Moreover, such programs should encourage individuals, families, and communities to embrace a broader understanding of stewardship as a faith response.

To ensure that annual giving programs remain consistent with the principles of stewardship, diocesan and pastoral staffs and volunteers should have significant ongoing opportunities for stewardship education and formation.

Capital Campaigns

A capital campaign is a carefully planned, well-organized needs-based program to raise a substantial amount of money within a specific time frame. Capital campaigns are ordinarily conducted to raise funds for major building or renovation projects. Occasionally, a campaign methodology may also be used to develop significant financial resources for other parish purposes (e.g., debt elimination, tuition assistance, or endowment development).

In a capital campaign, well-informed and well-trained volunteers visit other members of the diocese or parish to discuss the purpose of the campaign, describe the diocese's or parish's capital needs, and answer questions. They then invite individuals and families to make multi-year commitments to the campaign (in addition to their annual giving to the parish, diocese, or other church-related organization).

Capital campaigns represent one of the many choices that individuals and families have to make gifts of time, talent, and treasure to the Church.

ELEMENTS OF A SUCCESSFUL CAPITAL CAMPAIGN

A successful capital campaign should ordinarily include the following elements:

- **A situation analysis and case statement** that outline the current situation in the parish (strengths, weaknesses, opportunities, threats) and make the case

for major funding needs. This phase of pre-campaign planning is greatly assisted if the diocese or parish has an up-to-date pastoral plan.

- **A communications program** that seeks to help all members of the diocese or parish understand, accept, and make a commitment to the purposes for which the campaign is being conducted. Ideally, the communications plan will include (1) personal conversations with key individuals and groups; (2) meetings with staff, volunteers, and others as appropriate; (3) printed and audiovisual materials that state the case and show how diocesan or parish needs will be met, and (4) regular reports that keep members of the diocese or parish informed at all stages of the campaign. It is essential that this communications effort involve *listening* as well as talking. Major mistakes can be avoided if, at an early stage in campaign planning, diocesan and parish leaders are able to listen carefully to the concerns and suggestions of those who will be asked to participate in the campaign as volunteers or as donors. An openness to make reasonable changes in the case or in the campaign plans will go a long way toward creating a positive atmosphere for the campaign's success.

- **Identification of major gift prospects** for the capital campaign (and the development of pledge range charts showing the number of major gift prospects and range of gift amounts that are needed) should be initiated as part of the communications phase of the project. This will ensure that those identified as major gift prospects will have an opportunity to participate in this important communications phase of the campaign. This phase of the capital campaign should raise awareness about stewardship as a "faith response." It should also provide major gift prospects with significant opportunities for participation in and support of the mission and ministries of the Church.

- **Committed leadership.** The success of an intensive fund-raising campaign depends on the active involvement of the bishop or pastor, key diocesan and parish staff members, the appropriate consultative bodies (e.g., pastoral council, finance council, and stewardship committee) and other groups as appropriate. In addition, there will be a need to recruit strong volunteer leaders to help plan and implement the campaign.

- **A detailed, well-organized campaign plan.** A successful capital campaign requires careful planning and discipline. Campaign planning starts with the situation analysis and includes the gathering of background materials, financial projections, and other important data. Once these resources have been assembled and a case statement has been drafted and communicated to prospective volunteers and donors (as described above), the diocese or parish is ready to undertake a feasibility study, the process normally used to determine whether an organization has the resources (and the commitment) necessary to raise the desired funds.

If the feasibility study results are positive, the diocese or parish is ready to recruit volunteer solicitors, establish detailed procedures and strict timelines, and develop the necessary procedures for cultivating prospects, soliciting gifts, and recording, acknowledging, and collecting campaign pledges.

Dioceses and parishes that seek to raise more than $1 million in a capital campaign should consider obtaining professional fund-raising counsel to conduct a feasibility study and/or supervise the organization and implementation of the campaign. Before engaging professional counsel, dioceses and parishes should interview three or more firms (including the person who will be designated as campaign director) and contact the references provided by each firm. Careful advance screening can help dioceses and parishes learn from the experiences of others and avoid costly and time-consuming mistakes in their choice of professional counsel.

CAMPAIGN TIMETABLES

Campaign timetables should be planned that do not conflict with parish or diocesan stewardship programs or annual appeals. In consideration of the many demands that are made on diocesan and parish staff and volunteers, it may be advisable to combine a capital campaign with the diocese's or parish's annual giving program. When this is the case, extraordinary care must be taken to make sure that prospective volunteers and donors know why the two efforts are being combined. In addition, in a combined annual and capital campaign it is especially important to emphasize that stewardship involves gifts of time and talent as well as gifts of treasure.

STEWARDSHIP AND THE CAPITAL CAMPAIGN

A diocesan or parish capital campaign will be consistent with the principles outlined in *Stewardship: A Disciple's Response* if the campaign plans and procedures respect the themes and convictions of the bishops' pastoral letter and if the campaign materials and other communications reinforce the teaching and practice of stewardship as a way of life. To ensure that a capital campaign is based on, and reinforces, a diocese's or parish's stewardship education program, campaign staff and volunteers should have a thorough acquaintance with the theology and practice of stewardship before campaign plans are designed or implemented.

Planned Giving

The term "planned giving" is now commonly used to describe commitments made by donors to transfer capital assets (including cash, stock, certificates of deposit, real estate, or other forms of personal property) to a qualified religious, educational, or charitable organization. Most of the time, a planned gift is made by means of a formal agreement or contract and the principal or income from the gift is not available to the organization until the terms of the agreement are fulfilled (usually at the death of the donor or spouse). Planned gifts are normally made from the contributor's accumulated assets as part of an overall estate plan. In addition to the normal benefits of charitable giving, planned gift agreements frequently result in tax advantages or other income benefits to the donor.

The most common form of planned gift is a bequest provision in a will. Other forms of planned giving include charitable trust agreements, gifts of real estate or insurance, charitable gift annuities, and various combinations of these individual agreements (technically known as "deferred gift agreements").

CHARACTERISTICS

The most distinctive characteristics of planned giving are the following:

- Gifts are made from capital assets in contrast to outright gifts that are normally made from the donor's current income.

- The donor's personal and financial objectives are of primary concern in the decision whether to make a planned gift and what form of planned gift agreement to choose.

- Depending on what form of planned gift agreement is chosen, the organization designated as the beneficiary may have to assume administrative and/or fiscal responsibilities (which would not ordinarily be the case in an outright gift).

As a result of the growing awareness of the importance of endowment as an essential source of support for religious, educational, and charitable organizations, a natural affinity exists between planned giving and endowment development. Because planned gifts are usually gifts from the donor's accumulated assets, it is not unusual for the donor to prefer some form of endowment or capital purpose that will "preserve" the gift in perpetuity.

PLANNED GIVING SEMINARS AND EDUCATIONAL PROGRAMS

Many dioceses and parishes now sponsor seminars and other educational programs for individuals and families interested in learning more about planned giving. Frequently, these educational programs are conducted by local attorneys and other professionals who are knowledgeable in this increasingly complex field and who understand the special requirements of church law. Copies of informational brochures and other planned giving resources are available from the National Catholic Stewardship Council and from firms that specialize in marketing and training for planned giving.

Efforts to provide individuals and families with information about planned giving should be integrated into the diocese's or parish's overall stewardship education program. If properly presented as a means of exercising responsible stewardship of their accumulated assets and as an opportunity to make a distinctive contribution to the mission and ministries of the Church, an educational program designed to promote planned giving can be a double service to church members. It can remind them of their overall stewardship responsibility and, at the same time, provide very practical suggestions on how to increase income, save taxes, and contribute to the Church.

Personal contact with planned gift prospects by a representative of the Church who is knowledgeable in the field of planned giving and who is sensitive to the prospects' needs is the best way to encourage planned gifts. It can also be a significant service to individuals and couples who need assistance in estate planning.

LEGAL AGREEMENTS

Because many planned gifts include agreements that legally bind the beneficiary or that may require administrative or fiscal management, all dioceses, parishes, schools, and other church-related organizations should check with the appropriate church authority before signing any agreements or contracts that would legally bind the organization under the provision of civil or church law.

ENDOWMENT FUNDS

Parishes and schools should not set up separate legal entities for endowment purposes without first receiving permission from their local bishop. A growing number of dioceses have now established diocesan foundations whose primary purpose is to acquire, manage, and invest endowment funds for the benefit of parishes, schools, and other church-related organizations. In these foundations, endowments are managed by investment professionals under the supervision of the local bishop. Individual funds are commingled to maximize the benefit to all. For more information about endowment funds, dioceses and parishes are encouraged to contact the National Catholic Stewardship Council or the Diocesan Fiscal Managers' Conference.

IV. Promoting Gifts of Time, Talent, and Treasure to the Parish and Diocese: Seven Steps to Success

The mission and ministries of the Church in the United States require the personal participation in and financial support of the Catholic people. The following suggestions are intended as a seven-step process (or checklist) to help bishops, pastors, and their staffs and volunteers successfully promote gifts of time, talent, and treasure to the parish and diocese in a manner consistent with the theology of stewardship and principles of effective development.

Step 1: Personal Witness

Since stewardship is a way of life, and not simply a program of church support, the most important ingredient in any effort to encourage giving of time, talent, and treasure is the personal witness of individuals (clergy, religious, and lay) who have experienced a change of heart as a result of their commitment to stewardship. For this reason, parishes and dioceses are strongly encouraged to ground their stewardship and development programs in the personal witness of the bishop, pastor, parish or diocesan staff, and volunteers. An example of this type of personal witness would be for the presider at a liturgy to make a financial contribution or complete a commitment card for time, talent, or resources.

Parish stewardship programs currently in use in parishes and dioceses throughout the United States provide excellent examples of clergy and lay witness talks that can be offered during the liturgies leading up to a stewardship or commitment weekend. To ensure that stewardship is seen as more than simply the parish's annual giving program, witness talks on stewardship themes should also be offered at various times throughout the year. Similarly, diocesan annual giving programs and other diocesan events should include opportunities for personal witness on the part of the bishop and others to the importance of stewardship as a faith response. It is also important that parish leaders present the parish financial report at a different time, preferably a few months prior to the sacrificial giving presentation.

Step 2: Commitment of Leadership

The personal commitment of the bishop or pastor is absolutely necessary for the success of diocesan and parish stewardship and development efforts. In addition, wherever possible, parishes and dioceses should have active stewardship committees whose members include a representative group of pastoral and lay leaders willing to pray, discuss, learn, and lead.

The leadership team commissioned by the bishop or pastor should be responsible for (1) stewardship formation and educational programs in the diocese or parish, and (2) oversight of the parish's or diocese's efforts to promote gifts of time, talent, and treasure for annual, capital, and endowment purposes. Professional staff and/or consultants should be employed where appropriate and where diocesan or parish resources permit.

As in all aspects of church life, the collaborative leadership and active involvement of many people are essential to the success of parish and diocesan stewardship efforts.

Step 3: Hospitality, Evangelization, and Outreach

Communities known for the vitality of their faith and for the quality of their service to people in need invariably inspire others to participate in their ministries and to be generous in their financial support. With this in mind, parishes and dioceses that seek to promote gifts of time, talent, and treasure to support the mission and ministries of the Church should first demonstrate that they are welcoming communities with a commitment to preaching the Gospel and serving the needs of others.

Parishes and dioceses should not make commitments to hospitality, evangelization, and outreach simply because this will enhance their ability to recruit volunteers or raise money. These activities should be the natural outgrowth of a parish's or diocese's mission. However, dioceses and parishes that seek to increase participation or to raise additional funds would do well to look to the effectiveness of their efforts to welcome, evangelize, and serve.

As an integral part of their commitment to stewardship as a way of life, parish and diocesan leaders should initiate and implement stewardship projects unrelated to the Church itself, e.g., conservation of natural resources, environmental improvements, advocacy projects to benefit the poor and needy, custody of family values, etc. In addition, as a witness to the value of generous giving that is not based on obligation or need, dioceses and parishes should try to make donations of time, talent, and treasure to people and causes (in their local communities and throughout the world) that are over and above their participation in assessments and second collections.

Step 4: Communication and Education

All the stewardship and development programs currently in use in dioceses and parishes throughout the United States require the use of one or more communications media. Printed materials, audiovisuals, telemarketing programs, computerized tracking and record keeping, and other contemporary communications instruments now complement letters from the bishop or pastor, witness talks, bulletin announcements, posters, and other traditional means of communication.

Given the competition that exists today for people's time and attention, parishes and dioceses that wish to be successful in stewardship and development must pay careful attention to the effectiveness of their communications. Especially since most dioceses and parishes are working with very limited communications budgets, the choices that are made about how to most effectively "tell our story" or "make our case" can be crucial to success. With this in mind, parishes and dioceses are urged to seek the assistance of qualified communications professionals (staff and volunteers) to develop communications plans that will make the best possible use of available resources.

Step 5: Recruiting, Training, and Recognizing Gifts of Time and Talent

The demands made on people's time and energy make it more important than ever to recruit, train, and recognize gifts of time and talent for the parish or diocese. Active recruitment of volunteers is essential to the parish's or diocese's stewardship of its own human and financial resources because the active involvement of individuals, families, and communities in the mission and ministries of the Church is one of the surest signs of the health and vitality of any faith community.

To make sure that the time and talent of volunteers are respected and used wisely, dioceses and parishes should invest staff time and budget resources in the training and continuing education of volunteers. They should also find appropriate ways to recognize and celebrate the precious gifts of time and talent that people contribute to the Church on behalf of the mission of the Church.

New educational resources and training materials are needed to help parishes and dioceses improve their efforts to recruit, train, and recognize volunteers. To ensure that gifts of time and talent receive their proper emphasis and are not overshadowed by efforts to secure gifts of treasure, careful attention should be paid to this increasingly important aspect of a total stewardship education program.

Step 6: Stewardship of Treasure

Parishes and dioceses that wish to encourage financial gifts for ongoing programs, capital needs, and endowment should look first to steps 1 to 5 above.

- Has the parish or diocese effectively witnessed to the value of stewardship as a way of life?

- Is the leadership fully committed to stewardship and development?

- Are individuals and families in this diocese or parish actively involved in ministries of hospitality, evangelization, and service?

- How effective are parish or diocesan communications?

- And, finally, are gifts of time and talent really welcome, or does the parish or diocese unwittingly send a message that it only cares about money?

The parish or diocese that can honestly evaluate itself on these questions with a positive result will be in an excellent position to encourage gifts of treasure to support the mission and ministries of the Church. Building on this kind of solid foundation, the diocese or parish should employ fund-raising methods that respect and reinforce stewardship themes of gratitude, accountability, generosity, and returning to the Lord with increase.

Within a total stewardship context, parishes and dioceses should not hesitate to use the best available ethically sound fund-raising practices to ask the Catholic people to make financial contributions that are planned, proportionate, and sacrificial. Provided that the basic approach is consistent with the theology and practice of stewardship, the principles and techniques of professional fund raising can be extremely helpful to the overall stewardship and development efforts of the parish or diocese.

Step 7: Accountability

Success in the stewardship and development efforts of a parish or diocese requires a visible commitment to accountability. This commitment includes accountability for the full range of parish or diocesan activities—from the way decisions are made and carried out by diocesan or parish personnel to the way money is collected, managed, and used. Indeed, accountability is fundamental to good stewardship.

Parishes and dioceses are urged to prepare annual reports of their stewardship. These reports should be prepared in a manner that promotes understanding of the relationship between the ministries of the Church and the financial affairs of the parish or diocese. Church leaders should also use the annual report to render an account of their stewardship of human resources (personnel policies, just compensation, etc.), and their stewardship of church property and facilities.

A visible commitment to accountability will be reflected in the leadership styles and attitudes of the bishop, pastor, and all who have responsibilities for the human, physical, and financial resources of the diocese or parish. Like personal witness, a commitment to accountability is essential to building a solid foundation for a diocesan or parish stewardship program.

The seven steps suggested here are not intended to be an exhaustive list of all of the programs or activities that are required for success in promoting gifts of time, talent, and treasure. However, the experience of parishes and dioceses in many different regions of the country shows that if these seven principles are honored, the Catholic people will respond generously to the invitation to participate in the mission and ministries of their Church.

A Final Word: Gratitude to All Involved in the Ministry of Stewardship

This resource manual outlines well the challenge that parishes and dioceses are trying to address in responding to the pastoral letter, *Stewardship: A Disciple's Response,* issued by the National Conference of Catholic Bishops in November 1992. However, one final word needs to be added. It is the word of gratitude and appreciation to all those involved in the ministry of stewardship and development. We need to appreciate the women and men for whom stewardship is a ministry and a vocation. We need to recognize the gift of volunteer time, effort, and energy that so many people generously share with their dioceses and parishes.

In a special way, we acknowledge the pastoral leadership of our parishes and dioceses—bishops, pastors, pastoral ministers, and countless others. Their own commitment to stewardship creates the environment that will help our faith communities continue the mission and ministry of Jesus in today's world. To all those whose lives reflect the challenge of a disciple of Jesus through a commitment to stewardship, thank you for your witness of faith and generosity.

In the words of St. Paul to the Philippians, "I give thanks to my God at every remembrance of you, praying always with joy in my every prayer for all of you, because of your partnership for the gospel from the first day until now. I am confident of this, that the one who began a good work in you will continue to complete it until the day of Christ Jesus" (Phil 1:3-6).

Appendix: Key Concepts

The following definitions of key concepts and terms for stewardship, philanthropy, development, and fund raising are offered in order to identify the similarities and differences among these important concepts that are too often used interchangeably.

Accountability

Central to our understanding of stewardship and development is the concept of accountability. Dioceses, parishes, schools, and other church-related organizations that seek to develop urgently needed human and financial resources need to show that their programs and services truly "make a difference" in meeting the spiritual, educational, and social needs of the people they serve. They also need to give evidence of their long-term stability and growth potential to encourage investment. This is a basic requirement of stewardship and development—to render an account of the organization's use of the time, talent, and treasure entrusted to its care. As the demand for charitable giving grows (and competition increases), accountability will become an even more important indicator of whether an organization is "worthy of investment."

Communications

Making sure that the members of a parish or diocesan family are well informed in our world of mass communications and increasingly sophisticated information technology requires much more than articles in the diocesan newspaper, bulletin announcements, form letters, or occasional newsletters.

Quality communications is the result of hard work and careful planning. It also requires a significant financial investment by the diocese, parish, school, or other church-related organization. Today more than ever, important matters need to be communicated as personally as possible through individual and group meetings, personal letters and phone calls, and a full array of printed, electronic, and audiovisual support materials. In addition, given the mobility of our people today, informational items should be communicated frequently and in a variety of ways, so that those who miss one information source can still be reached through other sources.

If the desired outcome of our communications efforts is a community of people who understand, accept, and are committed to the mission and goals of the diocese, parish, school, or agency, we must develop forms of communication that can inform, motivate, and invite people to participate in our mission. As a Catholic community about to enter the new millennium, the communications opportunities and challenges that are being presented to us are staggering. The way we respond to these challenges and opportunities will have significant consequences for evangelization, religious education, and all our stewardship and development activities.

Development

Development refers to a program of planned or systematic growth in which a religious, educational, or charitable organization reaches out to its various publics and invites them to invest in its current and long-range goals. According to this definition, a successful development program involves the coordination and integration of three essential functions: planning, communications, and fund raising.

Fund Raising

Unlike stewardship, which is a way of life involving all aspects of an individual Christian's daily life, fund raising is a very specific set of activities designed to support the mission and goals of a diocese, parish, or other church-related organization. Fund raising is a discipline. It is a planned and organized effort to find potential volunteers and donors, to build strong relationships, and to ask for gifts of time, talent, and treasure to support the fund-raising organization's specific mission and goals. Although there are many different kinds of fund-raising activities, efforts to raise money for voluntary organizations fall into two main categories: direct fund raising and indirect fund raising.

DIRECT FUND RAISING

Prospective donors are directly asked to make a contribution of their time, their talent, and/or their treasure for the benefit of a religious, educational, or charitable organization. Direct fund-raising activities are normally organized into an annual appeal for unrestricted funds to support current programs and activities, special appeals for short-term or special projects, capital campaigns for building or other major projects, and planned giving (wills, trusts, real estate, etc.) that is sometimes associated with endowments.

The primary advantage of direct fund raising is its emphasis on building a strong, per-

sonal relationship between the donor and the organization that is seeking support. In each of the direct fund-raising efforts mentioned above, the organization seeking support must do careful planning, communicate its case in compelling and convincing ways, and "ask for the gift" in appropriate and effective ways.

Although most voluntary organizations use some combination of direct and indirect fund-raising methods, growing financial needs and increasing competition for the fund-raising dollar have caused organizations to rely less on indirect fund raising and to turn to more effective and efficient direct fund-raising methods.

INDIRECT FUND RAISING

Prospective donors are asked to purchase goods or services (magazines, candy, picnics, benefit dinners, etc.), and net profits are used to benefit a religious, educational, or charitable organization. These forms of fund raising often have very positive social benefits (e.g., building a stronger sense of community among staff and volunteers). However, the activities themselves do not necessarily build strong relationships between individual donors and the organization seeking support. Generally speaking, indirect fund-raising efforts are more effective at raising smaller amounts of money (often at little or no cost) than they are at raising substantial funds. Thus, if the goal is $500, an indirect fund-raising activity (e.g., bake sale) might be the perfect method. If, however, the goal is $50,000, an enormous amount of time, effort, and energy may be required to achieve this goal through indirect means.

Generosity and Self-Giving

In addition to the importance of accountability, what stewardship and development programs have in common is the basic underlying value or conviction that self-giving is good for the spiritual health and vitality of the individual, family, or community. In addition, all professional, ethically based fund-raising programs recognize that the needs of the human family compel individuals and groups to reach out beyond their individual homes, neighborhoods, or communities to help others who are in need and to make contributions to the common good that would not be possible otherwise.

As in any aspect of Christian life, we sometimes take the value of self-giving for granted, and we forget that raising funds should never be an end in itself. Thus, while it is important to keep in mind the significant differences that exist among the concepts of stewardship and development, it is also essential that we understand that these concepts are not compatible with tactics that seek to raise money through excessive pressure or guilt and are clearly incompatible with deception or fraud. In fact, when properly understood and practiced, the concepts of stewardship and development represent a tradition of generosity and service that should make any Christian and any citizen proud.

Philanthropy

Philanthropy can be defined as any voluntary action that benefits human society. Literally, philanthropy (which means "love of humanity") refers to a caring disposition that prompts individuals and communities to give of themselves with no other motive than the benefit of others. Like stewardship, philanthropy includes the concept of volunteerism, that is, gifts of "wisdom and work" as well as gifts of wealth. Among the distinguishing features of American culture are the philanthropic traditions that have

developed in all regions of the United States in response to community needs. In recent years, as government support has declined, education, social services, the arts, and many voluntary organizations have increasingly had to rely on the private philanthropy of individuals, corporations, and foundations. As a result, organizations like Independent Sector have been formed to remind all Americans that maintaining our country's tradition of philanthropy is not just the responsibility of a wealthy elite but is a civic duty to be shared by all. In the Greek Orthodox tradition, "philanthropy" is understood in a religious context and is very similar to our concept of stewardship.

Planning

To be successful in developing the human and financial resources needed to carry out its mission, a diocese, parish, school, or agency needs to have a plan. The purpose of the plan is to set direction by answering the following fundamental questions:

- Who are we? What is our primary mission?

- What makes us distinctive as a diocese, parish, or other church-related organization? What values do we choose to emphasize as characteristic of "what we stand for"?

- What do we want to do? What are our major long-term goals?

- How can we accomplish our goals? What are our main objectives?

- What specific action steps will we take to carry out our objectives? How do we measure our success or failure (accountability)?

A plan that can simply and honestly answer each of these fundamental questions will accomplish two important objectives: (1) it will set direction for all the programs and activities of the diocese, parish, or other church-related organization, and (2) it will guide all stewardship and development activities by setting the agenda for communications and establishing priorities for fund raising.

Role of Leadership

Successful stewardship and development programs require the active involvement of *all* of an organization's leaders (bishop, pastor, and other church leaders) working together as a team. As traditionally defined, the successful stewardship and development team requires the participation and interaction of leaders as follows:

EXECUTIVE *(bishop, pastor, and other executive staff)*
> Responsible for articulating the mission and goals; identifying opportunities for investment; planning; ensuring accountability; and soliciting major gifts.

VOLUNTEER LEADERS *(council or board members; other lay leaders)*
> Responsible for providing counsel and guidance on policy; representing community needs and interests to the organization; endorsing programs; validating resource needs; advocating for strong support within the community; and soliciting major gifts.

STAFF *(paid staff, such as diocesan development director, or volunteers)*
> Responsible for coordinating all stewardship and development activities, including stewardship educational programs; monitoring and updating long-range plans; developing and imple-menting communications strategies; organizing fund-raising efforts for annual, capital, and endowment purposes; and soliciting major gifts.

Depending on the size of the diocese, parish, or organization, these three leadership roles (executive, staff, and volunteer) will involve many staff members and volunteers whose active involvement in stewardship education and in various fund-raising programs is essential to the overall success of a development program. What the team concept illustrates is the fact that successful development is never the result of a single person (staff or volunteer) whose job is "to raise money." As an integral part of the stewardship responsibility of a diocese, parish, school, or agency, some aspect of the overall development function should be included in everyone's job description.

Stewardship

Who is a Christian steward? One who receives God's gifts gratefully, cherishes and tends them in a responsible and accountable manner, shares them in justice and love with others, and returns them with increase to the Lord.

Talent

If stewardship means taking care of, and sharing, all God's gifts, then stewardship of the gift of talent means nurturing, developing, and using the God-given abilities and characteristics that help to define "who we are" as individual human persons. Most of us know what it means to contribute money or to give away our precious time, but what does it mean to be a good steward of talent?

Our talents are the special blessings that each of us has received from a loving Creator who prizes the diversity and abundant variety of all creation. When we volunteer to work for our parish or diocese or to help a neighbor with a difficult chore, what we have to give is much more than our time. We also give something of ourselves, those characteristics that make each of us distinctive as human beings. We call these our "talents," those things that we're good at or that we especially like to do. When we volunteer to help others by sharing our talents with them, we give them something far more precious than our time or money. We give them something of ourselves, an intimate sharing of "who we are" for the good of others.

All of the parishes, schools, agencies, and institutions of the Church in the United States are blessed with thousands of volunteers who share their talents with others. The "time and talent catalogs" that many parishes publish each year describe hundreds of ways that people can and do give of themselves, from visiting the sick to frying fish, from counseling youth to serving on parish committees. These gifts of self are every bit as important as the financial contributions we make to support the Church's ministry.

Time

A true understanding of stewardship begins with taking care of and sharing the gift of time. Stewardship of time involves the realization that none of us "owns" time. Each of us is given only so much of it, and planning a careful schedule in order to have the time to work, to rest, to play, and to pray is vital in the stewardship of our physical, emotional, spiritual, and intellectual lives.

In a busy society like ours, time is one of the most precious possessions we have. How we spend our time is perhaps the clearest indication of our progress in a life of Christian discipleship.

Treasure

True stewardship is taking care of and sharing all that we have and all that we are—our time, talents, and treasure. Why is it so important to share our treasure?

Money and all of the things that we possess (our treasure) are gifts from God that we are asked to care for and generously share for our own benefit and the good of others. It is important for us to share our money and all of our material possessions for two reasons: first, because all the good things that God has made (including money) are meant to be shared, *   cond, because each of us has a *need to .*

Why do we need to give? We need to give our money to individuals and families in need, to the Church, and to other worthwhile charitable organizations because giving money is good for the soul and because we need to return thanks to a loving God for all of the many blessings each of us has received.

One of the most frequently asked questions in any stewardship educational program is "How much do I have to give?" The answer (from a stewardship perspective) is *nothing.* We don't *have* to give anything. "How much do we want to give?" is the question that stewardship asks. Stewardship is not minimum giving. It is maximum giving. That means giving as much as we can, as often as we can, from the heart as a faith response because we are generous stewards who want to share our time, talent, and treasure with others.

Frequently, in discussions of stewardship (or "sacrificial giving"), reference will be made to "the biblical tithe" (giving 10 percent of income) and other norms that could provide helpful guidelines for generous giving. As disciples of Jesus, each of us has a responsibility to support the Church and to contribute generously to the building up of the body of Christ. The emphasis in the bishops' pastoral, *Stewardship: A Disciple's Response,* is not on "tithing" (giving a fixed percent of income), but on giving according to our means. In many ways, this is a far more challenging norm. It challenges us to be good stewards not only in how much we give away, but in what we do with all our resources.